anythink

D0603826

Birds

Hawks

by Cecilia Pinto McCarthy

Consultant:
Tanya Dewey, PhD
University of Michigan Museum of Zoology
Ann Arbor, Michigan

CAPSTONE PRESS
a capstone imprint

First Facts is published by Capstone Press,
1710 Roe Crest Drive, North Mankato, Minnesota 56003.
www.capstonepub.com

Library of Congress Cataloging-in-Publication Data
McCarthy, Cecilia Pinto.
 Hawks / by Cecilia Pinto McCarthy.
    p. cm.—(First facts. birds)
 Includes bibliographical references and index.
 Summary: "Discusses hawks, including their physical features, habitat,
range, and life cycle"—Provided by publisher.
 ISBN 978-1-4296-8607-5 (library binding)
 ISBN 978-1-62065-215-0 (ebook PDF)
 1. Hawks—Juvenile literature. I. Title.

QL696.F32M33 2013
598.9'44—dc23
                                    2012002140

Editorial Credits:
Lori Shores, editor; Juliette Peters, designer; Kathy McColley, production specialist

Photo Credits:
Getty Images: Bloomberg/Daniel Acker, 21, Photo Researchers, 10–11, Photo Researchers/
Jim Zipp, 6; iStockphoto: Mark Coffey, 13; Minden Pictures: Foto Natura/Dietmar Nill,
17; Newscom: Design Pics/John Pitcher, 8, WLP, Inc./Douglas Graham, 20; Shutterstock:
Brad Thompson, cover, Brenda Carson, 19, Mircea BEZERGHEANU, 9, Pavel Mikoska,
1, 5, Steve Byland, 14

Artistic Effects
Shutterstock: ethylalkohol, Pavel K, pinare

Essential content terms are **bold** and are defined at the bottom of the page where they
first appear.

Printed in the United States of America in North Mankato, Minnesota.

042012   006682CGF12

Table of Contents

Hawk-Eyed Hunters

As hunters, hawks rule the skies. These **raptors** are built for hunting. Dark speckled feathers help them hide in the trees. Keen eyes notice faraway movements. Powerful wings speed hawks toward targets. Sharp **talons** grasp and kill small animals. Strong, hooked beaks tear at meat.

Hawk Fact!

The feathers on the face of a harrier hawk form a disk. This arrangement helps it hear animals moving on the ground.

raptor—a bird that hunts other animals for food

talon—a large, sharp claw

wings

eyes

beak

talons

red-tailed hawk

young Cooper's hawk

Large and Small

Hawks can be many sizes. Large hawks have **wingspans** of up to 5 feet (1.5 meters). The smallest hawks are only as big as robins. Their wingspans are about 20 inches (51 centimeters). Unlike most birds, female hawks are usually larger than males.

wingspan—the distance between the outer tips of a bird's wings

Forest Hawks and Soaring Hawks

Forest hawks watch for **prey** from high up in trees. Short rounded wings and long tails help them zoom around trees to catch prey.

Swainson's hawk

rough-legged hawk

Broad wings and short, wide tails help hawks **soar**. Soaring hawks circle high in the sky. Sharp eyesight helps them spot prey far below.

prey—an animal hunted by another animal for food

soar—to fly through the air without flapping wings

9

Just Meat, Please!

Hawks hunt during the day. They only eat meat, but they are not picky eaters. Hawks catch furry animals such as mice and rabbits. They also eat lizards and snakes. Hawks even snatch other birds right out of the sky.

Hawk Fact!

Most hawks hunt alone. Harris' hawks hunt in groups of up to six birds. They share the prey they catch.

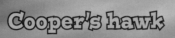
Cooper's hawk

Hawks around the World

   More than 50 kinds of hawks live around the world. They live on every continent except Antarctica. Hawks live in forests, grasslands, deserts, and mountains.

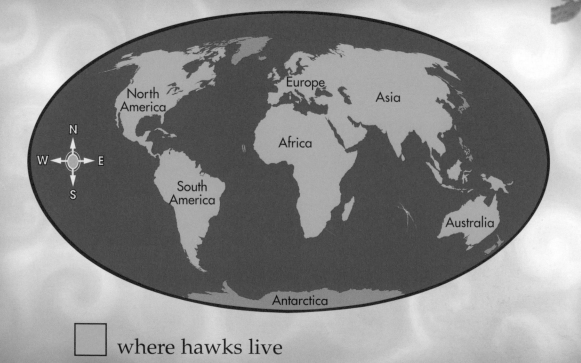

where hawks live

red-tailed hawk

Many hawks have **adapted** to live in towns and cities. Some hawks make their nests in parks. Other hawks nest on buildings or telephone poles.

adapt—to change behavior to fit in a new situation

red-tailed hawk

On the Move

Hawks that **migrate** may fly short distances or thousands of miles. Hawks use areas of moving warm air called **thermals** to soar easily. They can fly farther before getting tired. Groups of hawks travel the same routes every year.

Hawk Fact!

A large group of hawks in a thermal is called a kettle.

migrate—to move between areas in different parts of the year for food, shelter, and breeding

thermal—a rising current of warm air

15

Sky Dancers

Male and female hawks do a sort of dance before **mating**. They circle each other in the sky. Then they dive and lock talons. After mating, they build a nest to use for years. The mating pair will usually stay together for life.

Hawk Fact!

Northern goshawks build nests up to 4 feet (1.2 m) wide.

mate—to join together to produce young

northern harriers

A Hawk's Life

Female hawks lay two to six eggs. Most female hawks keep their eggs warm while males bring them food. Chicks hatch in about one month. Newborn chicks are weak and wobbly. Their parents feed them and keep them safe.

Hawk Fact!

Some hawks bring live animals to the nest to teach chicks how to hunt.

Life Cycle of a Hawk

Newborn: Newly hatched chicks have just a few soft feathers.

chick

Young: Some hawks have yellow eyes that turn orange or red as they grow.

Adult: Large hawks live 13 to 20 years. Smaller hawks live three to five years.

Leaving the Nest

When chicks are a month old, they practice flying. They stand and flap their wings. By six weeks, most hawk chicks **fledge**. Even though they can fly, fledged chicks stay in the nest for several more weeks.

red-tailed hawk

fledge—to learn to fly

Amazing but True!

A male red-tailed hawk named
Pale Male lives in New York City's
Central Park. Pale Male is famous
because he nests on a building. Since
1991 people have watched Pale Male
and his mate hunt and care for chicks
in his city home.

Glossary

adapt (uh-DAPT)—to change behavior to fit in a new situation

fledge (FLEJ)—to learn to fly

mate (MATE)—to join together to produce young

migrate (MYE-grate)—to move between areas in different parts of the year for food, shelter, and breeding

prey (PRAY)—an animal hunted by another animal for food

raptor (RAP-tur)—a bird that hunts other animals for food; raptors have hooked beaks and sharp talons

soar (SOR)—to fly without flapping wings

talon (TAL-uhn)—a large, sharp claw

thermal (THUR-muhl)—a rising current of warm air

wingspan (WING-span)—the distance between the outer tips of a bird's wings

Read More

Lundgren, Julie K.. *Hawks*. Raptors. Vero Beach, Fla.: Rourke, 2010.

Marsico, Katie. *Hawks*. How Do We Live Together? Ann Arbor, Mich.: Cherry Lake Pub., 2010.

Norris, Ashley P. Watson. *Falcons*. Birds. North Mankato, Minn.: Capstone Press, 2013.

Internet Sites

FactHound offers a safe, fun way to find Internet sites related to this book. All of the sites on FactHound have been researched by our staff.

Here's all you do:

Visit *www.facthound.com*

Type in this code: 9781429686075

Index